@RosenTeenTalk

RACIAL PROFILING AND DISCRIMINATION

Danielle Haynes

ROSEN PUBLISHING
NEW YORK

Published in 2021 by The Rosen Publishing Group, Inc.
29 East 21st Street, New York, NY 10010

First Edition

Editor: Elizabeth Krajnik
Designer: Michael Flynn
Interior Layout: Rachel Rising

Photo Credits: Cover, p. 1 Riccardo Piccinini/Shutterstock.com; Cover Cosmic_Design/Shutterstock.com; Cover, pp. 1, 6, 8, 10, 12, 16, 18 ,20 ,22, 24, 26, 30, 32, 34, 36, 40, Vitya_M/Shutterstock.com; pp. 3,5 Monkey Business Images/Shutterstock.com; pp. 3,15 Westend61/Getty Images; pp. 3, 29 photokup/Shuttestock.com; pp. 3, 7, 24, 39 Prostock-studio/Shutterstock.com; pp. 3,45 kali9/ E+/Getty Images; p. 6 Rawpixel.com/Shutterstock.com; p. 8 DEREK HENKLE/AFP/Getty Images; p. 9 Ekaterina_Minaeva/Shuttetrstock.com; p. 11 Mihajlo Maricic / EyeEm/Getty Images; p. 12 Alex Potemkin/E+/Getty Images; p. 16 William Lovelace/Hulton Archive/Getty Images; p. 18 Valery Sidelnykov/Shutterstock.com; p. 19 Print Collector/Hulton Archive/Getty Images; p. 20 rblfmr/Shutterstock.com; p. 22 Michael Dechev/Shutterstock.com; p. 23 Scott Olson/Getty Images News/Getty Images; p. 25 Bloomberg/Getty Images; p. 27 Andrew Burton/Getty Images News/Getty Images; p. 29 photokup/Shutterstock.com; p. 30 Spencer Platt/Getty Images News/Getty Images; p. 31 Motortion Films/Shutterstock.com; p. 32 Klaus Vedfelt/DigitalVision/Getty Images; p. 33 Yellow Dog Productions/The Image Bank/Getty Images; p. 34 track5/E+/Getty Images; p. 35 Jon Feingersh Photography Inc/DigitalVision/Getty Images; p. 37 ymgerman/Shutterstock.com; p. 40 Paul Craft/Shutterstock.com; p. 41 Halfpoint/Shutterstock.com; p. 42 Sean Locke Photography/Shutterstock.com; p. 43 MARK RALSTON/AFP/Getty Images.

Some of the images in this book illustrate individuals who are models. The depictions do not imply actual situations or events.

Cataloging-in-Publication Data

Names: Haynes, Danielle.
Title: Racial profiling and discrimination / Danielle Haynes.
Description: New York : Rosen Publishing, 2021. | Series: RosenTeenTalk | Includes glossary and index.
Identifiers: ISBN 9781499468182 (pbk.) | ISBN 9781499468199 (library bound)
Subjects: LCSH: Racism--United States--History--Juvenile literature. | Race discrimination--United States--History--Juvenile literature. | United States--Race relations--History--Juvenile literature.
Classification: LCC E184.A1 H39 2021 | DDC 305.800973--dc23

Manufactured in the United States of America

CPSIA Compliance Information: Batch #BSR20. For further information contact Rosen Publishing, New York, New York at 1-800-237-9932.

CONTENTS

Chapter 1

Singled Out

One of my favorite things to do after school is to meet up with friends at a local coffee shop. We hang out, study, drink tea, and eat snacks.

Sometimes I'm the first one to arrive. I usually wait for my friends before I order anything.

Today, I used the bathroom and studied while I waited. I was minding my own business when a couple of police officers came in and told me it was time for me to leave. They said I was causing a problem.

A new worker had called the police because she said the bathroom is only for paying customers. Why didn't she talk to me first? Why did she call the police? I think the shop worker singled me out because of my race.

Nicole is mixed race. Her father is white and her mother is black.

WHAT IS RACIAL PROFILING?

Racial profiling is when law enforcement or security officials target a person because of their race. This may also include **ethnicity**, **religion**, or **nationality**. These officials include police officers, security guards, and even some airline pilots. The law enforcement officials don't target the person because they've broken the law or show that they might break the law.

Just because someone looks or acts different from other people doesn't mean they're a criminal. We should celebrate our differences and learn more about our peers.

Every day, people of all races and ethnicities break the law in the United States. But racial profiling means certain people are more likely to be questioned or arrested than others.

EXAMPLES OF RACIAL PROFILING

Racial profiling can happen to people of all races and ethnicities. But usually it happens to people who are in the minority where they live or are visiting. In the United States, that means people are often targeted for:

- Having a skin color other than white
- Speaking a language other than English
- Appearing to practice a certain religion

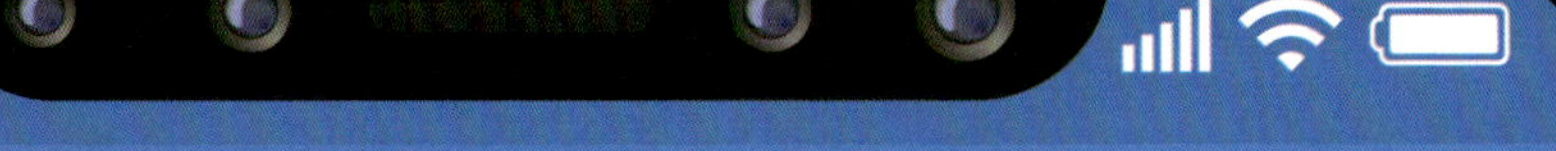

WHY RACIAL PROFILING IS A PROBLEM

Racial profiling is a problem because it unfairly targets people based on how they look.

In 2017, the Department of Justice believed that the Chicago Police Department did things that went against the Fourth **Amendment**.

When police use racial profiling, people of color are more likely to be arrested, jailed, and fined. It leads to more people of color having criminal records. This can cause many problems in life.

Many jobs check into your past. It can be hard to get a job if you have a criminal record.

Unconstitutional

The U.S. **Constitution** lays out the laws and system of government. An amendment is a change in wording or meaning in a law, bill, or motion. Racial profiling goes against the Fourth Amendment of the U.S. Constitution. That section states that police have to have a good reason to search or arrest someone.

FACTS AND FIGURES

- Police shoot 3.5 times more unarmed black people than unarmed white people.
- Police are more than twice as likely to use force against black and Hispanic people than white people.
- In Oakland, California, 28 percent of the population is black. But 60 percent of police stops involve black people.
- About the same percent of white and black people use drugs in the United States. Black people are more than twice as likely to be arrested for it than white people.

Local-level crime rates don't explain racial **bias** in police shootings. However, individual police officers' racial bias may be a factor in police shootings.

LIVING WHILE BLACK

African Americans are often the target of racial profiling. White people sometimes call the police on black people who are doing normal, noncriminal activities. The callers do so just because they think African Americans aren't supposed to be in that place.

In 2018, a golf course worker called police on five black women for golfing too slowly.

The practice of stopping African Americans for no good reason has given rise to the phrase "living while black." It can be frustrating for people to always worry about whether the police might confront, or question, them. After all, we're all just trying to do the same things and live our daily lives.

EXAMPLES OF LIVING WHILE BLACK

In 2018, the police were called on African Americans who were:

- Waiting for a friend inside a coffee shop
- Shopping for clothes
- Knocking on doors for a **political** campaign
- Helping the homeless
- Swimming in a pool
- Mistakenly mowing the wrong lawn
- Visiting a gym
- Grilling at a park
- Moving into a new home
- Asking for directions

Chapter 2

Feeling Like You Don't Belong

Last year, my family moved to a gated community. I was so nervous about going to a new school and living in a new town. But we were lucky because there was a pool only for people who lived in the gated community. Swimming is one of my favorite activities, and now I could swim whenever I wanted!

My sister and I decided to go to the pool after we unpacked. The water felt great. But not long after we go there, a woman who was there with her two kids said we had to leave. She said the pool was only for **residents**. We told her we'd just moved in, but she said she'd call the police. She said we didn't belong there.

Racial profiling means that sometimes people assume someone's breaking the rules just because they're a different race, ethnicity, or religion from most people in that area.

SLAVERY AND SEGREGATION

When the United States first **declared** independence from Great Britain in 1776, people had already been enslaving Africans for over 100 years. In 1865, the 13th Amendment to the U.S. Constitution abolished, or did away with, slavery.

Martin Luther King Jr. (center) was a leader of the civil rights movement. King and others fought for equal rights for African Americans in the United States.

But even after this, black people in the United States had limited rights. Black men didn't have the right to vote until 1870. The government passed laws that segregated, or separated, black people from white people in public spaces, including schools, restaurants, trains, and even prisons.

A TIMELINE OF RACISM IN THE UNITED STATES

1619: The first enslaved Africans are brought to the colonies.

1776: The United States declares independence from Great Britain.

1865: The 13th Amendment abolishes slavery.

1896: The Supreme Court rules that facilities for African Americans can be "separate but equal."

1954: The Supreme Court rules segregation unconstitutional.

1964: The Civil Rights Act outlaws **discrimination** based on race and other things.

1965: The Voting Rights Act outlaws racial discrimination in voting.

RACIAL PROFILING AND SLAVERY

In the early days of the United States, the color of a person's skin, not their actions, could get them in trouble with the law.

Before slavery was abolished, enslaved people weren't allowed to leave their owner's property unless they had **permission**. If a police officer saw a black person walking freely in public, the police officer could stop them. Slaves had to show **proof** they were allowed to leave the owner's property. Later, free black people had to show their freedom papers.

Who Was Harriet Tubman?

In 1849, Harriet Tubman escaped a Maryland **plantation**. She fled to the North and then worked in the Underground Railroad. This was a network of mostly black people who helped enslaved people escape from the South to the North and Canada. There they'd be free. Tubman helped hundreds of people escape slavery. She knew how hard slavery could be and risked her life to help others.

Harriet Tubman and the Underground Railroad helped many **fugitive** slaves reach freedom. But the Fugitive Slave Act meant former slaves and free black people could be captured in the North and sold back into slavery.

STOP AND FRISK

Today, even though there's no slavery, some police departments still have **policies** that allow law enforcement officials to use racial profiling to try to catch criminals. Some police departments use what's called a Terry stop or stop and **frisk**.

Many people of color have **protested** the NYPD's policy of stop and frisk. Stop-and-frisk policies may go against people's constitutional rights.

These policies allow officers to stop and search anyone they think might have carried out a crime, might be in the process of carrying out a crime, or might be about to carry out a crime. Most people stopped are **innocent**. Police tend to stop more people of color than white people.

NEW YORK CITY'S STOP-AND-FRISK STATISTICS

A lot of people don't like the New York Police Department's stop-and-frisk program. They say NYPD officers unfairly target people of color. NYPD officers have stopped using it as much.

At the policy's height of use in 2011, of 685,724 people stopped:

- 605,328 (89%) were innocent
- 350,743 (53%) were black
- 223,740 (34%) were Latinx
- 61,805 (9%) were white

In 2018, of 11,008 people stopped:

- 7,645 (70%) were innocent
- 6,241 (57%) were black
- 3,389 (31%) were Latinx
- 1,074 (10%) were white

IMMIGRATION

Sometimes racial profiling goes beyond the color of a person's skin. Law enforcement officials may target people because they look like they come from a different country. Other people are targeted because they look like they practice a different religion.

Some **immigration** laws push police to check people's **identification**, even if the person isn't breaking the law. What might make a law enforcement official think someone isn't a U.S. citizen? The color of their skin? The language they speak?

Border Patrol officers often carry out stop-and-frisk policies near the border. They stop people to check if they're citizens of the United States. They don't always catch people who've crossed the border illegally.

How the U.S. Border Patrol Uses Racial Profiling

Checkpoints: Officials check the citizenship of certain drivers at locations near the border.

Patrols: Officials pull over drivers they think are breaking immigration laws.

Buses & trains: Officials ask passengers their immigration status.

Workplace raids: Officials show up at a factory or business to check the citizenship of workers.

RELIGION

After the September 11, 2001, terrorist attacks, the U.S. government began stopping, questioning, and holding people against their will based upon their national origin, their ethnicity, and their religion. Law enforcement officials mostly looked for young men who appeared to be Arab, Muslim, or South Asian.

Law enforcement officials arrested thousands of people, many of whom were innocent. Some were questioned as possible terrorists. Others were deported, or forced to leave the country because they weren't U.S. citizens. This caused many people to distrust law enforcement.

On January 29, 2017, in Washington, D.C., many people protested President Donald Trump's travel ban on five Muslim-majority countries—Iran, Libya, Somalia, Syria, and Yemen.

MUSLIM PROFILING

The government targets people who practice Islam by:

- Segregating them in prisons
- Watching their communities
- Getting them to spy on other Muslims
- Preventing them from boarding airplanes (No Fly List)
- Removing them from planes they've already boarded because someone thinks they're going to cause trouble
- Banning people from several Muslim-majority countries from entering the United States

KNOW YOUR RIGHTS

Getting stopped or **raided** by immigration officers can be scary. Whether you're a citizen or a **documented** or undocumented immigrant, it's important to know your rights.

- Don't panic or run away from officers.
- If you're a citizen, tell the officer.
- If you're a legal resident, always carry documents that prove it.
- Don't lie about your status or give fake documents.
- Don't sign anything without a lawyer's help.

Thousands of migrant adults and children have been held for long periods of time in cells in federal detention centers. They often don't have a place to wash their hands or shower and many people become sick.

END FAMILY
DETENTION!
-Responsible Endowments Coalition-

Chapter 3

What's Going to Happen?

Yesterday, my brother, sister, and I started to get worried when our mom didn't come home after work. She wasn't answering her phone. About an hour after she should've been home, I went to our neighbor's house. She works with our mom. Our neighbor told me that Immigration and Customs Enforcement officers raided the factory where she and my mom work. They arrested workers who couldn't prove they're U.S. citizens. Our mom was one of them.

We were so scared—especially my little sister. My mom was born in El Salvador. What'll we do if she's deported? I don't understand why ICE officers even raided the factory. Our mom wasn't doing anything illegal. She was just working like everyone else was.

ICE officers often raid workplaces known to have workers who are undocumented immigrants.

CONSEQUENCES OF RACIAL PROFILING

Racial profiling can make people feel a lot of emotions. In areas where racial profiling happens a lot, distrust can grow between police and members of the community. If people are always worried about the police unfairly targeting them, it can be hard to believe police will help when they're needed.

People who belong to groups that are commonly the target of racial profiling often deal with long-term health issues. That's partly because they're always worried the police may stop them.

People who distrust police may be less likely to ask them for help. A survey in 2018 found that white Chicago residents were more likely to reach out to police than black residents.

HOW RACISM MAKES PEOPLE FEEL

- Separated from their friends
- Like they have to act against **stereotypes**
- Like they have to represent their community
- Like it's hard to focus on school or work
- Fearful, frustrated, angry, or helpless
- Distrustful of law enforcement
- Like they have to work twice as hard to succeed

GETTING HELP

Being the target of racial profiling can cause a person to feel a lot of worry. It's good to have some tools for dealing with profiling—and discrimination in general.

People experiencing racial profiling and discrimination may be able to join a group of others in their community. There, people can talk and share stories about how they've been treated. Some people also seek **counseling**. Many schools have counselors who can work with students. If not, people can ask their doctor to help them find a counselor.

Some lawyers specialize in cases in which clients have been racially profiled or discriminated against.

LEGAL HELP

If you're the target of racial profiling or discrimination, there are legal groups that can help. They also provide information on their websites.

- American Civil Liberties Union (**www.aclu.org**)
- Southern Poverty Law Center (**www.splcenter.org**)
- Amnesty USA (**www.amnestyusa.org**)
- National Immigration Law Center (**www.nilc.org**)
- Muslim Legal Fund of America (**www.mlfa.org**)

WHAT'S A GOOD ALLY?

Whether or not you deal with it yourself, everyone has a part to play in stopping racial profiling. You should speak up against racism and be a good ally even if it doesn't affect you in the same way. An ally is a person who gives help to another person.

Stopping racial profiling and discrimination starts with you. Read about it to gather as much knowledge as you can. Talk to your friends about your experiences and theirs. Listen to how they feel.

An App to Help

The ACLU has created a mobile app to help everyone be a good ally. Use it if you think law enforcement officials are targeting someone unfairly. The app lets you take videos when police officers stop or question people. It sends the videos to the ACLU even if the police take your cellphone. Visit the ACLU website **(www.aclu.org)** to find the app for your state.

Being a good ally means sticking up for your friends, no matter the color of your skin.

TAKING A STAND

Sometimes doing the right thing means you'll have to take a stand. Here are some ways to stop racial profiling and discrimination:

- Call out racism when you hear and see it.
- Attend antiracism protests.
- Give money to organizations that fight discrimination.
- Be willing to speak up. But if you're not a person of color, be sure to let people of color lead.
- Think about your own biases and work to fix them.
- Vote for politicians who want to fight discrimination.
- If you can't vote yet, you can help on Election Day or donate to politicians' campaigns.

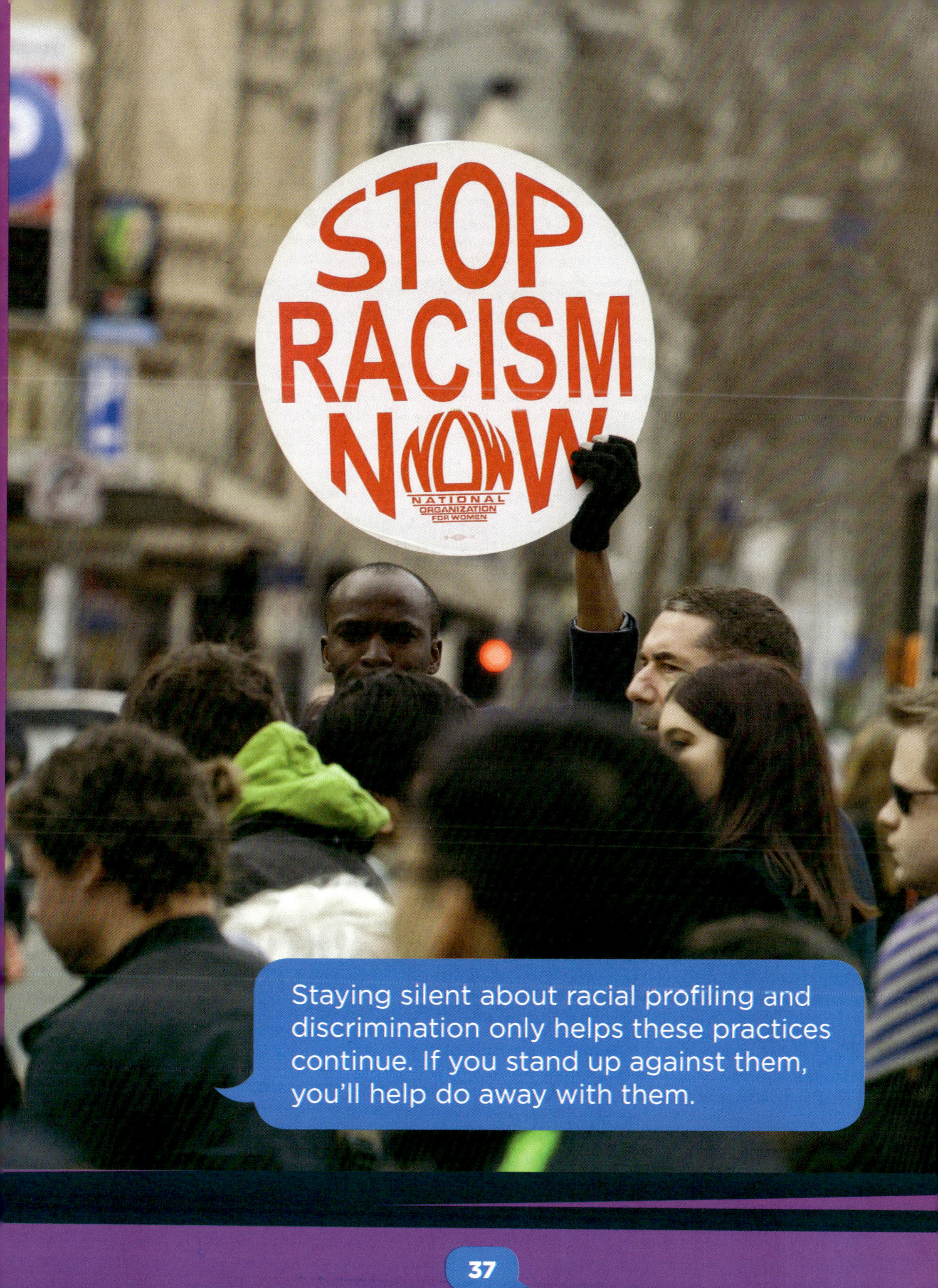

Staying silent about racial profiling and discrimination only helps these practices continue. If you stand up against them, you'll help do away with them.

Chapter 4

Doing What's Right

My best friend, Joe, and I got into a really big fight today. He was mad at me because I didn't say anything when the school resource officer blamed him for stealing chips at lunch. I know Joe didn't take them because I was with him the whole time. But I didn't say anything because I was scared.

Joe was upset because the officer often singles out the black and Latinx kids at school. He said I didn't understand what it's like because I'm white. He's right. I should've told the officer Joe didn't steal the chips.

I always thought it was good enough to just not be racist. But it's not. I shouldn't stand by quietly when someone is being unfairly targeted because of their skin color.

Being a good friend means listening to and **empathizing** with each other.

PEACEFUL PROTEST

Racial profiling can cause a lot of anger in communities. Sometimes there are situations that get a lot of attention in the news. The Black Lives Matter movement came about during a time when law enforcement officers shot a number of unarmed black people.

Protesting is a good way to get your message out there. Protests can involve marches and **rallies** at important places such as police stations or town halls. In the past, people have used nonviolent **civil disobedience** to protest racial profiling and discrimination.

Other Forms of Protest

Boycott: Don't shop at businesses that discriminate against people of color. Tell people why you won't be shopping there anymore.

Walk-out: Leave school or work as a large group at a certain time to draw attention to your cause.

Write: Reach out to politicians who serve your town or city and tell them you support laws banning discrimination.

Share: Tell your peers why racial profiling is bad and share experiences with it. Post about it on social media.

There are many nonviolent ways teens can protest against racial profiling.

GETTING RESULTS

In recent years, police departments have responded to protests about police shootings of unarmed people of color. They've made changes to their policies to protect innocent people.

Some, like the Los Angeles Police Department, keep track of information about their traffic stops. They want to see if officers are unfairly pulling over more people of color. Many police departments have started using body cameras. This gives the government proof of how law enforcement officers treat people. Training sessions help police officers more easily recognize racial profiling.

Still Work to Do

Even though people have worked hard to end racial profiling and discrimination, these practices still exist. On July 31, 2019, the Senate introduced the End Racial and Religious Profiling Act. It would prohibit federal, state, and local law enforcement from targeting a person based solely on race, ethnicity, national origin, religion, gender, gender identity, or sexual orientation without trustworthy information that links the person to a crime. It would also require police departments to increase data collection, participate in training, and create policies about profiling.

In 2020, leaders in Los Angeles County, California, addressed racial profiling linked to the spread of coronavirus and worked to stop misinformation about the illness. Because the virus originated in China, many people wrongly accused Asian Americans of spreading the illness.

Chapter 5

Making a Change

I was really upset that the coffee shop worker and police officers singled me out. I wasn't doing anything wrong! I told the police officers I was waiting for my friends and that I usually visited the coffee shop at least once a week. My friends from school showed up and backed me up.

We sat down with the police officers, worker, and coffee shop owner to talk about what happened. The worker apologized to me. The owner recognized my friends and me. She promised to make her current and future employees take an antiracism training course.

The police officers told me their police chief had already planned some bias training for their department. I'm really glad everyone listened and understood my point of view. I know a lot of people aren't so lucky.

GLOSSARY

amendment: A change in the words or meaning of a law or document, such as a constitution.

bias: A tendency to believe that some people, ideas, etc., are better than others, which often results in treating someone unfairly.

civil disobedience: Refusal to obey laws as a way of forcing the government to do or change something.

constitution: The basic laws by which a country, state, or group is governed.

counseling: Advice and support that is given to people to help them deal with problems, make important decisions, and more.

declare: To say or state something in an official or public way.

discrimination: Unfair treatment based on factors such as a person's race, age, religion, or gender.

documented: Having documents, or official pieces of paper that give information about something, such as citizenship.

empathize: To share the same feelings as another person.

ethnicity: A sense of common ancestry based on cultural attachments, past linguistic heritage, religious affiliations, claimed kinship, or some physical traits.

frisk: To search a person quickly for something that may be hidden.

fugitive: A person who runs away or tries to escape.

identification: Something that shows who a person is, such as a driver's license or passport.

immigration: The act of coming to a country to settle there.

innocent: Not guilty of a crime or other wrong act.

nationality: A group of people who share the same history, traditions, and language, and who usually live together in a particular country.

permission: The approval of a person in charge.

plantation: A large area of land, especially in a hot part of the world, where crops such as cotton are grown.

policy: A law that people use to help them make decisions.

political: Of or relating to politics or government.

proof: Something that shows that something else is true or correct.

protest: To gather together to show strong disapproval about something, or an event at which people do so.

raid: To make a surprise attack on someone or something.

rally: A public meeting to support or oppose someone or something.

religion: An organized system of beliefs, ceremonies, and rules used to worship a god or a group of gods.

resident: A person who lives in a place.

stereotype: A commonly held idea about a group of people that isn't necessarily true.

INDEX